PICTORIAL
KING'S LYNN
PAST & PRESENT

EIGHTH CENTENARY YEAR 2004

BY VERA WITT

ISBN No.: 0-9513119-4-8

CONTENTS

ACKNOWLEDGEMENTS.
INTRODUCTION.

Town Of King's Lynn 1
South Gate & London Road 3
Millfleet 6
Tuesday Market Place 10
High Street 20
Streets Of King's Lynn & Rastrick Map 28
Norfolk Street 33
Broad Street & St Dominic Square 41
New Conduit Street 49
Tudor Rose Restaurant 56
St. Nicholas Chapel & Exorcist's House 57
Austin Street, Austin Fields 63
& 1929 Map
North End 74
Frederick Savage 84
Our Borough & Map 89
Filling In Of The Loke 91
Fisher Fleet 95
King's Lynn Docks 99
Common Staithe Quay & Conservancy Board 06
Highgate Bridge & Hob in Well 119
Kettle Mills 122
Highgate 126
Cattle Market 130
King's Lynn Railway 133
Blackfriars Street & Baxters Plain 139

St. James Chapel & St. James Park 146

Red Mount & The Walks 153

Greyfriars Tower & Park 159

Theatre Royal Cinema 163

Greenland Fishery 165

St. Margarets Place & St. Margarets Lane 167

St. Margarets Church 171

Town Hall 176

Queen Street & Baker Lane 179

Fleets & Waterways 182

Explorers Of Lynn 191

Purfleet Street 195

The Bankhouse King Staithe Square 198

South Quay 200

Boal Quay 204

St. Georges Guildhall 206

Bibliography 208

ACKNOWLEDGEMENTS

To the people named below I would like to express my sincere gratitude for their assistance in obtaining photographs from their photographic collections for my book, for without their help this book would not have become possible.

Lynn News.   Eastern Daily Press.   Conservancy Board.
Associated British Ports.
Dick Goodchild.
Chris Boxall.
J. Walker.
J.Witt.
David Pitcher.
King's Lynn Borough Council Archives
Jim Jude.
James Tuck.
L. Watts
Mrs. B. Taylor
J. Patten.
N. Whittle   www. Fenprint.com.
M&GN Circle.
King's Lynn Central Library for 1929 Map.
Ordnance Survey Department Southampton.

©Vera Witt 2004
First Printed 2004
Published By Alver Books.
Printed by King's Lynn Press Ltd, Austin Fields King's Lynn

INTRODUCTION

With the writing of my other books on King's Lynn I discovered that like myself many people are also interested in our historic Town, there is so much history yet to be uncovered. King's Lynn is unique from its very earliest beginnings.

In this book I have decided to show King's Lynn mainly in picture form, although it does contain some informative text, but most of the book is from the view of the photographer, not only of the past but also of the present day. With the reading and viewing of my book, I hope it will encourage the readers curiosity to find out more of King's Lynn's vast amount of history which is fascinating to discover, as I found out for myself.

View of King's Lynn.

THE TOWN OF KING'S LYNN

The main entry into the Town is via the South Gate that is situated on London Road, the roadway was constructed in 1803-6.

The South Gate is the only remaining gateway that still stands. The gate was originally a bretask (wooden tower), it was rebuilt and stonefaced in 1437.

The pedestrian side arches were not incorporated into the gate until the 19th century.

Another gateway into the Town from Norwich was the East Gate via the village of Gaywood, (Gaywood remained a village until it was incorporated with King's Lynn in 1935). The East Gate was built 1327-1377, as part of the Town's fortifications, (both the East Gate and South Gate were originally wooden structures).

The East Gate archway was not high enough for some transportation, this led to it being demolished in 1800, some of the stonework is incorporated into the gateway of Hillington Hall. Beyond the East Gate to the east was pasture and marshland known as Rondeshill. Another gate spanned the Dowshill Fleet in the 14th century. The earlier structure of Highgate Bridge which is next to the site of the East Gate can still be seen beneath the present day one. The remains of the Town wall fortifications can still be seen in Littleport Terrace and Kettlewell Lane.

Lynn was built on the shore of the Lin, a lake which gradually diminished with the many years of salt panning, this led to the silting up of the foreshore, thus forming the foundations of Lynn. More and more land was reclaimed and Lynn soon began to expand into a larger Town. Newland or Terra Nova at the North End of the Town (later named North End) was also built as more land was reclaimed, so one can say that Lynn evolved from the sea.

The earliest building in Lynn was the original St. Margarets Church built on the foreshore in 1101 by Bishop Herbert de Losinga 1054-1119. It was of a simple Norman style, very little remains of the original church, only the base of the south west tower. The present day church was rebuilt in the 13th century with a spire.

The Town over the centuries from its early mention in the domesday book 1086 was known as Lenne Episcopi or Bishops Lenne. In September 1204 during the reign of King John the town was granted its first charter, making it a free borough. This charter also gave the Port of Lynn special powers for waterborne goods. (In this year 2004 Lynn will celebrate the eight hundred years of the charter).

In 1537 Henry VIII removed the town from the Bishops jurisdiction and renamed it Lynn Regis or King's Lynn.

The Town has undergone many significant changes, not only in architecture but also with substantial expansion.

Early South Gate & Honest Lawyer. Courtesy of the Fenprint Collection.

South Gate showing the Honest Lawyer.

Entry into King's Lynn via South Gates. The roundabout has been altered since this photograph was taken.

MILLFLEET

The Millfleet was still a waterway through to the Walks when the construction of London Road began, so before the building of the road the only route into town from the south was via the South Gates, Southgate St., Friars St., Bridge St. and Church St.

Horse drawn coaches left enroute to London three days a week from the Crown Inn in the Southgate ward, although coach transport left from other departure points, the Dukes Head on the Tuesday Market Place being one.

A corn mill was situated near Ladybridge, the entrance being in Nelson St., this mill was closed and converted into flats in the 1960's. A water mill was on the fleet near the Greyfriars Monastery, due to the shortage of water it was then converted into a windmill, later a coal and tar works was on the site.

St. Margarets School was opened in 1844 and closed as a school in 1970, (now St Margarets Social Club).
The Lincoln Tavern was built in 1846, (now a private house).
The Ancient Jewish Cemetery is also on the Millfleet, it was opened in 1830 by Hart Jones a silversmith in High St., although some of the graves are of an earlier date probably prior to 1811.
The Cemetery was closed in 1841 but it is still attended to.

In 1290 during the reign of Edward I the Jewish community who lived mostly in Jews Lane were driven from the town, later Jews Lane was renamed Surrey St. to deny the existence of the community in this area, during Cromwells rule they returned in small numbers. The Jewish synagogue was in Tower St. in 1811.

By 1813 it had been taken down and a Methodist chapel built on the site. The Millfleet was piped and filled in from Ladybridge to London Road in 1898.
The Carnegie Public Library on the corner of London Road and Millfleet was opened in 1905, it is now King's Lynn Central Library .

King's Lynn Central Library.

Early King's Lynn Library. Courtesy of the Fenprint Collection.

The Millfleet showing the old Corn Mill at Ladybridge. Converted into flats in the 1960's.

Tuesday Market Place showing the fountain and lamp. They were erected on the site of the Market Cross in 1858. The lamp was taken down in 1925.

Early Tuesday Market Place. Courtesy of the Fenprint Collection.

Dukes Head Hotel, built for Sir John Turner 1685. Named after the Duke of York, later James II. Henry Bell was the architect.

Early opening of King's Lynn Mart. Courtesy of J. Walker.

13

Big Wheel on Lynn Mart.

Two Wheels on Lynn Mart in the 1980's.

King's Lynn Mart 2003. Courtesy of Lynn News.

Passing Out Parade giving the Freedom of the Borough to the R.A.F. on Tuesday Market Place.

Maydens Head, Tuesday Market Place.

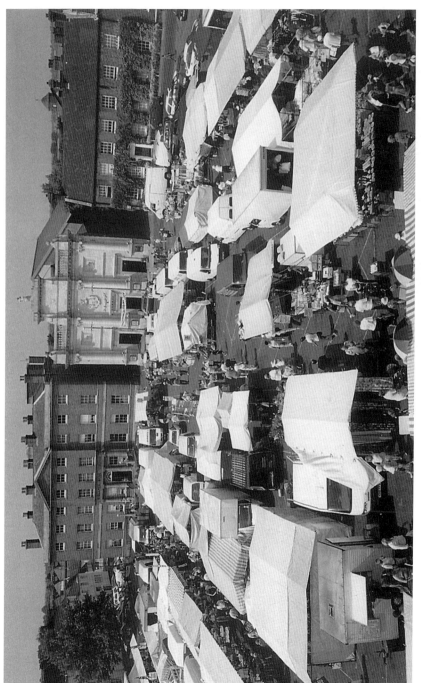

Market Day, Tuesday Market Place. Courtesy of Lynn News.

Early High Street.

High Street, 1968.

David Greig, High Street.

Scott & Son, High Street. Demolished, now Boots the Chemist. Courtesy of James Tuck.

23

Boot the Chemist, High Street, present day.

High Street from the Tuesday Market Place, present day.

High Street looking towards Tuesday Market Place, 1960's.

High Street looking towards Tuesday Market Place, present day.

STREETS OF KING'S LYNN

The names of the streets that we know today are very different from those of yesteryear, some familiar ones that we walk along in our daily lives, for example Norfolk St., High St., Broad St., New Conduit St., King St., Blackfriars St., Queen St., Austin St., and Pilot St.

In the book I have enclosed Rastrick's Map of 1725 and have written a list of the streets as they were and are now.

No's

1   Clow Lane (Blackfriars St.)
2   Sedgeford Lane
3   Mad Lane (Union Lane)
4   Codlin Lane (Tower Place)
5   Miln Lane (Stonegate St.)
6   Crooked Lane (Now part of Hillington Square)
7   Priory Lane
8   St. Margarets Lane
9   College Lane
10 Little Wingate (Baker Lane)
11 Common Staithe Lane (Ferry St.)
12 Pudding Lane (Water Lane)
13 Page Stair Lane
14 Pillory Lane (Market Lane)
15 Drews Lane (North St.)
16 Hopmans Way (Austin St.)
17 Butchers Row/Jews Lane (Surrey St.)
18 Spinner Lane (Paradise Lane)
19 Baxter Row (Tower St.)
    Northirne (St Anns St.)
20 Leeds St./Skinner Row (St James St.)
21 Coldhirne St. (Bridge St.)
22 Lath St. (Nelson St.)
23 Wingate St./Bulwer Row (Queen St.)
24 Little Staithe Square (King Staithe Square)
25 Checker St. (King St.)

26 Purfleet St.
27 Briggate
28 Mercer Row } All Part Of High St.
30 Cooks Row

31 Fincham St. (New Conduit St.)
32 Websters Row (Broad St.)
33 Listergate St. (Chapel St.)
34 Woolmarket/Woolpack St. (St Nicholas St.)
35 Dowshill (Pilot St.)
36 Gresemarket St. (Norfolk St., between Broad St. and High St.)
37 Damgate (Norfolk St. from Broad St. to Littleport St.)
38 Littleport St.
39 Clow Bridge (Junction of Blackfriars St. & Railway Road)
40 Baxters Bridge (was on Baxters Plain)
41 Old Gannock Bridge
42 Bevers Bridge (was over Millfleet)
43 Ladybridge (is over the Millfleet)
44 South Gate
45 High bridge (was over Purfleet on High St.)
46 Purfleet Bridge
47 Dowshill Bridge (was over Fisher Fleet)
48 Hopmans Bridge (was in Austin St.)
49 Littleport Bridge (was at junction of Austin St., Littleport St. and Blackfriars Road)
50 East Gate Bridge.

Rastrick Map 1725 overleaf.

A
PLAN
OF THE
BOROUGH
OF
KING'S LYNN
DRAWN BY
WILL.ᴹ RASTRICK
M DCC XXV.

GUNTERS SCALE of 20 CHAINS.

5   10   15   20

WEST PROSPECT OF KINGS LYNN.

River Gaywood

Norwich Road

RIVER

REGALIA.

ARMS of LYNN.

44 London Road

Wisbeach Road

Lynn River or Saudingham EA.

Z

K

K

Z

Y

T

B

S

H

L

E

P

M

O U S E

CHURCHES AND PUBLIC BUILDINGS

A. St. Margarets Church.
B. All Saints Church.
C. St. Nicholas Church.
D. St. James Workhouse.
E. Grammar School.
F. Austin Friars.
G. Blackfriars.
H. Whitefriars/Carmelites.
I. Greyfriars Tower.
K. Red Mount.
L. Guildhall. (Town Hall).
M. Custom House.
N. Hospital for Old Men. (Paradise House).
O. Tuesday Market Place.
P. King Staithe Quay.
Q. Common Staithe Quay.
R. St. Anns Fort.
S. Oil Mill. (Millfleet).
T. Water Mill.
U. Water Engine. (Kettle Mills).
W. Fish Ponds. (Old Fort St. Ann).
X. East Gate.
Y. South Gate.
Z. Fortifications. (Old Town Wall).

Early picture showing Taylor Seed Merchants, Norfolk Street. Courtesy of Mrs. B. Taylor.

Norfolk Street after pedestrianisation.

View from Railway Road of the part of Norfolk Street which was demolished to make way for John Kennedy Road.

Co-operative Society, Norfolk Street. Now site of Lidl Store.

Lidl Store, showing John Kennedy Road junction at Norfolk Street, present day.

Norfolk Street from Broad Street showing Q.D. on left, present day.

Norfolk Street from Broad Street towards High Street, present day.

Norfolk Street from High Street, present day.

Baths Yard, Broad Street, now part of the Vancouver Car Park. Old Electric Theatre in background. Courtesy of J. Jude.

41

Broad Street, 1960's showing Empire Cinema. Courtesy of James Tuck.

Broad Street in the 1960's.

Broad Street from Norfolk Street, present day.

Broad Street, present day, before re-development 2004. Courtesy of Lynn News.

Broad Street from Baxters Plain, present day, before re-development 2004.

Broad Street from Baxters Plain, present day, before re-development 2004.

St. Dominics Square, present day, before re-development 2004.

Early New Conduit Street.

49

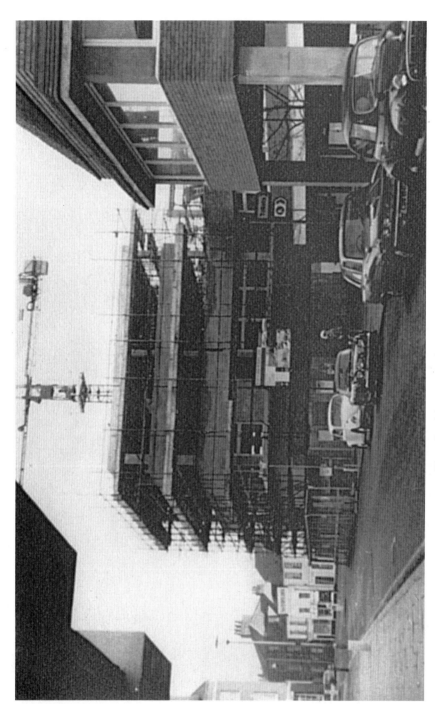

New Conduit Street before pedestrianisation.

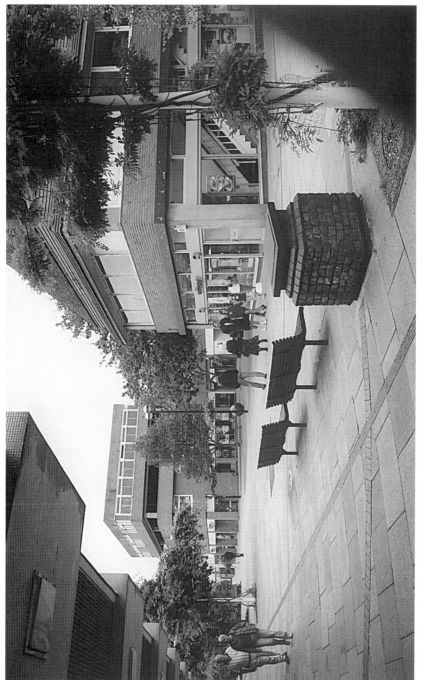

New Conduit Street, present day before re-development 2004.

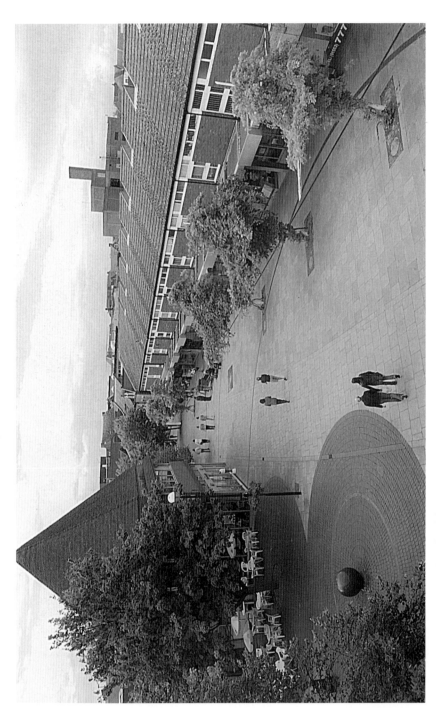

New Conduit Street, present day before re-development 2004. Courtesy of Lynn News.

New Conduit Street, present day before re-development 2004.

New Conduit Street, present day before re-development 2004.

New Conduit Street, present day before re-development 2004. Courtesy of Lynn News.

Tudor Rose restaurant.

ST. NICHOLAS CHAPEL

Bishop William Turbus (de Turbe) 1095-1174, built St. Nicholas Chapel in 1146 mainly as a chapel for the fishing community of North End who lived mostly in Pilot St., North St. and North End Yard.

Many owned and worked their own fishing boats, although there were many families I have named only a few eg, Bone, Bunting, Bailey, Witt, Bouch, Newby, Fisher, Balls, Leman, Carter, Chase, Bunn and Castleton.

St. Nicholas Chapel was where many of these families were baptised, married and had their burial service, today the Chapel is only used for burials primarily of those with connections to old North End.

St. Nicholas Chapel. Courtesy of J. Walker.

St. Nicholas Chapel Porch, also showing part of the tomb believed to be
that of a 14th century prior.

St. Nicholas Chapel Porch.

St. Nicholas Chapel, present day.

Chapel Lane showing side view of St. Nicholas Chapel and end of Exorcist's House.

Originally the Exorcist's House. now a private dwelling.

AUSTIN STREET & AUSTIN FIELDS

Before the construction of John Kennedy Road the usual route from the north end of town into Austin St. was via North St., St Anns St., Chapel St., although this was not the quickest way, Pilot St., and Chapel Lane were shorter.

Turning left from Chapel Lane, Austin House stood on the corner, it was the home of Marshall the coal merchant, next the home of the Roper family (these two buildings still remain), Shaws shop and Garden Nursery, the M&GN Traffic Managers building and garden named the Priory, built circa 1880, it was closed in 1936 as the M&GN offices. During the war it was used for the billeting of American personnel, later it became the Post Office Engineering Depot (now site of Regis House and Priory House).

The Electricity Sub Station remains (sited beside John Kennedy Rd). Next to the sub station were allotments and a field where cattle grazed these backed onto the Dock Railway line. A stream bordered by trees flowed through the field and made its way into the Gaywood river at Kettlewell lane via a sluice, (the site is now Austin Fields Industrial Estate).

The Co-operative Bakery & Dairy (now King's Lynn Joinery), the old Co-op Stables (now used by Ward & Gethin Solicitors) and six houses still remain.

Many Houses and Yards were on the right side of Austin St., the St. Augustine Labour Club stood on the corner of Chapel St. and Austin St., (now Kings Court Council Offices occupy the site). Albert St., left side from Austin St., East St. and Johnsons Square, Garland Yard, Austin Place, Hope Yard and Houses along Austin St., were all demolished (now Car Park). Railway Passage which gave pedestrian access through to Norfolk St. and Railway Road disappeared with the construction of the new road, Andrews Chemist Shop, Hairdressers and East & Co Rope Manufacturers in Norfolk St., were also demolished).
The Co-operative Warehouse and yard (now Lidl car park).

Austin Street before demolition. Courtesy of Lynn News.

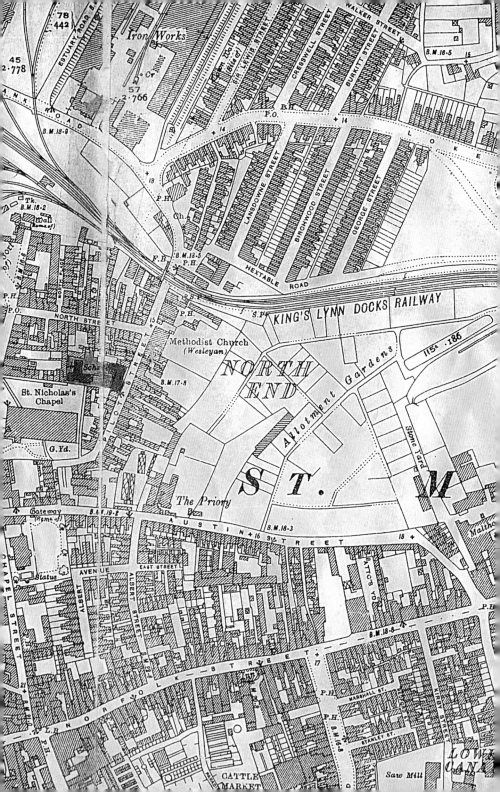

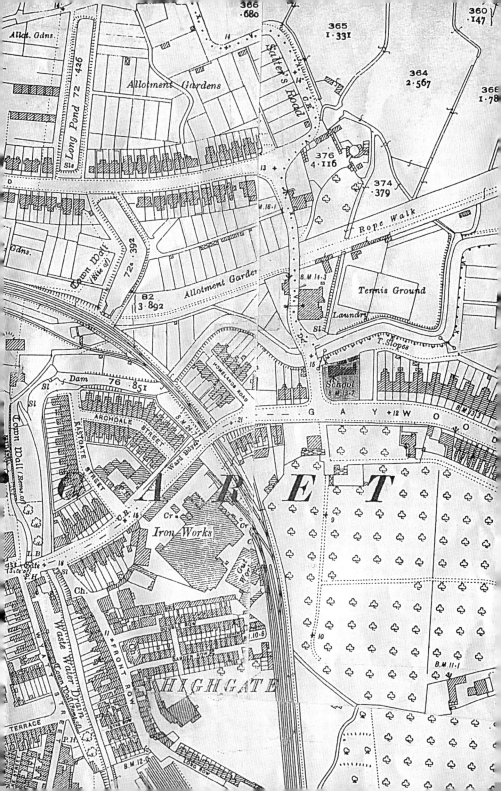

M&GN Traffic Managers Office. Courtesy of the M&GN Circle.

Austin House, one of the few remaining houses in Austin Street.
There are a few at the Littleport Street end, these are all that still stand
after the demolition of North End.

Albert Street, looking towards Norfolk Street. Courtesy of James Tuck.

Austin Street Car Park before Regis House was built.

Austin Street Car Park, present day.

Austin Fields Industrial Estate.

View of North End before demolition. Courtesy of the Eastern Daily Press.

A North End marriage on the 4th September 1871, showing the families of Fisher, Bailey, Cockerill and Reed-Green.

Children of North End.

Fishermans Arms, demolished with North End clearance. Courtesy of L. Watts.

Harts Yard, Pilot Street also demolished with the North End clearance. Courtesy of J. Jude

Watsons Yard, North Street. Demolished with the North End clearance. Courtesy of J. Jude.

Remains of Pilot Street, present day.

View of Pilot Street after clearance of North End.

Grampus House in Pilot Street, originally the Grampus Public House. Licensees in 1871-72 were John and Jane Witt, my husbands great grandparents.

Block Houses, Old Fisher Fleet. Demolished with the building of the Bentinck Dock.

83

FREDERICK SAVAGE

Frederick Savage was born in 1828, he died in 1897 aged 69 years, there is a monument to his memory in the Hardwick Road Cemetery, his wife is also buried with him, she died in 1899.

He started his engineering business in Tower Street, but with the necessity for bigger premises he expanded the iron foundry on the site of the old St. James Workhouse after it was demolished, at a later date he moved to St. Nicholas St.

In 1872 he purchased reclaimed land after the course of the river was altered with the digging out of the Estuary cut which was started in 1850, completed in 1853 (the river as we know it today). This was before the Loke, a waterway was filled in. Afterwards the road we know as Loke Road and the streets on the northern side were built.

In 1873 he founded the St. Nicholas Ironworks, also building a house for his family on the site circa 1874. He was a notable man who became Mayor of Lynn in 1889, a statue was erected in his honour on London Road.

He was famous for his patent of the galloping horses on the carousel that for many years have thrilled children on the Lynn Mart.

The Ironworks remained until 1973 when warehouses were then built on the site. The house seen by people passing on their way to the Docks and Fisher Fleet was also demolished at a later date, only a small part of the original wall of the Ironworks remained on the corner of Loke Road.

There was a commemorative plaque upon the wall. Sadly these were removed in 2003 as the whole site is now under redevelopment, but Frederick Savage will not be forgotten as the new development is to be named ST. NICHOLAS PARK, and the plaque will be on one of the buildings.

The monument of Frederick Savage on London Road. Unveiled 27th May 1882.

Frederick Savages' house before construction of Bentinck Dock

Frederick Savage driving a chain driven traction engine in about 1870.

Frederick Savage's Gallopers built in 1920 at Savages Ironworks, King's Lynn.

OUR BOROUGH
OLD LINES OF FORT ANN

On the old map of the borough are marked the lines of Fort Ann, in 1624 it was named the Outwork. By looking at the map it shows that the Loke waterway was within the lines. The Long Ponds in the early map are shown to be within the lines, but on the 1929 map the dotted line shows that they were outside the fort. By writing this I wanted to show the places that were eventually built within the lines of Fort Ann.

Sir Lewis St., Cresswell St., 1897, Burkitt St., 1896/97, Walker St., Rope Walk where East & Co the rope manufacturers had premises in Johnsons Brickyard, Fairlawn Estate which were mostly allotments, part of Woodwalk Avenue, Edma St., Turbus Rd., Anderson Close and houses along the left hand side from John Kennedy Rd., all the above were built after the filling in of the Loke which took ten years to complete.

The Bentinck Hotel public house and streets on the right side eg, Victoria Hotel public house, (now a clinic), Sunday School, (now a double glazing firm) North End Yard occupied before 1841, Landsdowne St., Birchwood St. These properties had been built and occupied by 1881. George St., was built a little later although some houses were in existence by 1896, built for Frederick Savage as homes for his workers at the St. Nicholas Ironworks.

At the bottom right hand corner of the Fort towards Kettle Mills other properties were built after 1929, Harewood Parade, Harecroft Parade, Harecroft Gardens and Harecroft Terrace.

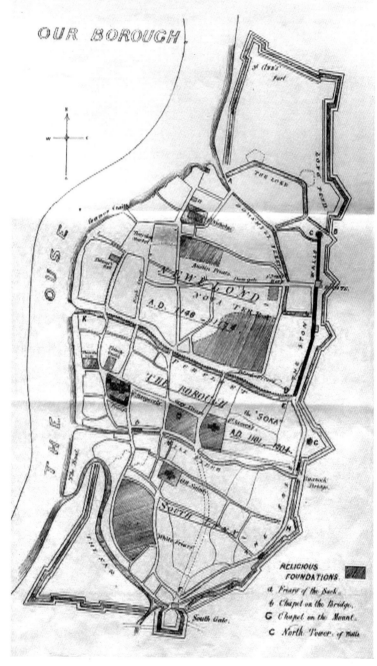

Old Map of the Borough.

FILLING IN OF THE LOKE

Date 1878. The Loke, it was reported as to the foul state of the water and that it should be cleansed out near the waterworks.

Date 13th March 1879, western end of Loke to be filled in, four feet above present water surface as far as the earth will suffice, but sloping off the bank on the north side of the Loke and throwing the earth there from into the Loke, but taking care at the same time not to injure the trees on the bank.

Date 9th Feb 1881, unemployed men to be set on to fill in part of the Loke pond with earth from the mound next to the Long Pond.

Date 17th June1881, filling in of Loke confirmed.

Date 9th Nov 1882, Mr G.H. Jewell complained about the footpath from the waterworks on the north side of Loke to North End, and of the want of a playground for the children of North End.

Date 9th May 1883, that the filled in part of the Loke at the North End and land adjacent belonging to the corporation be offered as building leases, a roadway not less than forty feet in width being set out on the site of the Loke.

Date 16th Oct 1884, Loke filled in at North End to a level with the adjoining ground, leaving the greater part of it a stagnant piece of water.

Date 1886, further filling in of Loke.

Date 1888, proposed gas lighting for Loke Road.

Taken from Council Minutes of the Hall Books in the King's Lynn Borough Archives.

Reference No.: K/C7/21.

The foreground of the photograph shows the North End of today built after the filling in of the Loke.

The Bentinck Hotel, Loke Road built 1883, known as the New Hotel, renamed the Bentinck Hotel in 1903.

Bentinck Arms, present day, (earlier as Bentinck Hotel).

View of old Fisher Fleet before the Bentinck Dock was constructed.

King's Lynn Fisher Fleet. Courtesy of L. Watts.

Fisher Fleet.

King's Lynn Fisher Fleet, present day.

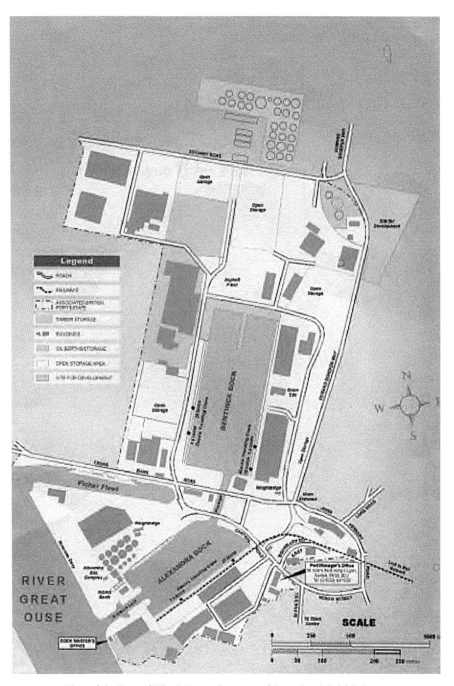

Plan of the Port of King's Lynn. Courtesy of Associated British Ports.

99

Early view of the Bentinck Dock showing coal chute.

Early Alexandra Dock. Courtesy of the Fenprint Collection.

Early Alexandra Dock. Courtesy of J. Walker.

Bentinck Dock.

Bentinck Dock. Courtesy of Conservancy Board.

View of docks taken from grain silo on Bentinck Dock.

View of Common Staithe Quay.

Common Staithe Quay after alteration.

Construction of Trinity Quay flats, Common Staithe Quay.

PILOT OFFICE & CONSERVANCY BOARD

King's Lynn being a Town of maritime importance from early times was not without its fortifications. Guarding the entrance to the harbour was St. Anns Fort situated at the northern end of the town, it had a battery of cannon that faced seaward.

The Pilot Office with a tower was built on the fort, the tower was a lookout that monitored shipping as they sailed towards Lynn. The river Great Ouse was subject to shifting sandbanks, this necessitated the use of Trinity Pilots to guide vessels into port.

The old Pilot Office was demolished when the course of the river was altered in 1853, because the fort was no longer on the waterfront. This resulted in a new Pilot Office being constructed on the Common Staithe Quay in 1856, a tower was added in 1864.

In Dec 1889 the SS. Wick Bay ran aground while sailing towards Lynn, attempts to save the vessel were to no avail, she was a total loss after breaking her back, thus causing a hazard to shipping using the port of Lynn. The Wick Bay had to be removed, the King's Lynn Corporation then in charge for the navigation of shipping into Lynn were responsible for her removal. This led to the forming of the King's Lynn Conservancy Board in 1897 by act of parliament, for the safety of all shipping and removal of any wrecks. Later the Board also became the Pilotage Authority.

The Conservancy Board has responsibility for the navigational markers and buoys in the shipping channel to the port. The Board operates two fast pilot cutters the "United" and the new "St Ann" to transfer the pilots to and from ships in the channel. The Board also give emergency towage cover into the port. Three other boats they operate are the new tug "Conservator" the "Staplewear" a survey vessel and tug when required and the "St. Edmund" for the maintainance of and placing navigational aids in the channel. They maintain forty buoys and eleven beacons which are in the approach channel. The approach was changed from Teetotal Channel (this was between Daseley Sand and the Thief Sand) the main channel is the Bulldog Channel (between Blackguard Sand & Stylemans Middle). Older channels were, Daseleys Sled (between Seal Sand/Daseley Sand), Corkhole (between Stylemans Middle & Peter Black Sand) the Old Lynn channel (between Thief Sand & Hull Sand).

The Conservancy Board has jurisdiction over extensive areas of the foreshore, salt marsh, wildlife and shellfish beds. The Wash is a conservation, marine site and a nature reserve.

Without the Conservancy Board the Port of King's Lynn could not function like it does today.

"SS Wick Bay". Courtesy of Conservancy Board.

Conservancy Offices, Common Staithe Quay. Courtesy of Conservancy Board.

The Conservancy Board offices built in 1856 on the Common Staithe Quay after the alteration of the river in 1853.

Pilot Cutter "United". Courtesy of Conservancy Board.

New Pilot Cutter, "St. Ann". Courtesy of Conservancy Board.

The new tug "Conservator". Courtesy of Conservancy Board.

"Staplewear" survey vessel also used as tug when required. Courtesy of Conservancy Board.

"St. Edmund" maintains navigational aids in the channel. Courtesy of Conservancy Board.

View of mouth of the River Great Ouse, taken from the grain silo. The River Great Ouse flows into the Wash, the Wash flows into the North Sea, (known in earlier times as the German Ocean).

Early print of Highgate Bridge. Courtesy of J. Walker.

Hob in the Well public house early 1900's.

Hob in the Well, present day.

KETTLE MILLS

In early times King's Lynn received its fresh water supply from the Gaywood River. In the 15th century the Kettle Mill was built by the side of the river on what was known as "Lazar Hill". At first the water was conveyed via open channels, at a later date it was carried by means of conduits into the town, these consisted of wooden piping bored from the trunks of trees. Due to the leakage of the pipes the supply became scarce, this resulted in the residents taking their water from the open fleets.

At a much later date a windmill was erected, the water was raised from the Gay (Gaywood River) by barrels to a wooden reservoir in a round tower in the town wall. Sometimes horses were used or an artificial waterfall which worked a machine called a water engine, this old engine became inadequate, so a new engine was installed in 1780. Although the new engine worked quite successfully it was decided by the council to replace it with a steam engine, unfortunately the price of coal and repairs made it uneconomical to continue its use. This caused the council to revert back to the water engine.

In 1829 a circular tower and engine house was built, the water was stored in the tower and pumped by a powerful steam engine. Cast iron mains were laid to transport the water into the town.
By 1863 a newer engine was installed to give a substantial water supply to all of the citizens, where before only those in the position to pay were supplied.

The cleaning out of the river was not carried out sufficiently, this resulted in a serious outbreak of typhoid fever in 1892. This prompted a new source of water being found for the town, which was unpolluted, thus spelling the demise of the Kettle Mill as the water supply.

Later the Kettle Mill was used as an electricity generating works for the borough, although the old water tower and chimney remained until the early 1970's. The building was demolished and the King's Lynn Drainage Board Offices now occupy the site.

Kettle Mills. Courtesy of J. Walker.

Electricity Generating Station built on site of the old Kettle Mills which was demolished. The Drainage Board office now occupies part of the site. Courtesy of James Tuck.

124

Remains of the Town Wall built 1294.

Front Row, Highgate before demolition.

Front Row, Highgate, present day.

Early Highgate Infants School, opened in 1877. Courtesy of J. Walker.

Highgate School, present day.

The old Cattle Market. Courtesy of Lynn News.

Bus Station in the 1980's.

131

Bus Station, present day.

KING'S LYNN RAILWAY STATION

The Railway Station was opened in 1846, the building was of a wooden construction. Initially the line was from Lynn to Downham Market, in 1847 it was extended to Ely and London.

In 1862 a line was opened to Hunstanton, this made it possible for members of the Royal family to visit their newly purchased Sandringham Estate. Edward prince of Wales (later Edward V11) was the first to use the Estate as a country retreat. The Hunstanton line closed in 1969.

In 1871 the foundation stone for the new brick building was laid. In January 1915 a bomb was dropped near the Royal train carriage shed when the town was attacked by Zeppelin air ships.

The late fifties and sixties saw the fazing out of steam locomotives, which were replaced by diesel and diesel electric power. In 1992 King's Lynn railway became fully electrified.

Early Railway Station. Courtesy of J. Walker.

Railway Station, present day. Note alteration to frontage.

Royal Train carriage shed almost hit by Zeppelin bomb in 1915.

Diesel Electric locomotive entering King's Lynn Station. The diesels' suceeded the steam locomotive in the late fifties and early sixties. In 1992 the railway became electrified.

The last steam train to ever arrive at King's Lynn Station November 2002. Courtesy of Lynn News.

137

Morrisons and Matalans now stand on the site of the goods yard and locomotive depot.

BLACKFRIARS STREET

The Clow Fleet on the 1725 map shows that it flowed from the Purfleet, under Baxters Bridge and the Clow Bridge towards the Walks and ran alongside Clow Lane. In 1866 when the Clow Fleet was piped and filled in, Clow Lane became Blackfriars Street and South Clough Lane.

The Stepney Baptist Chapel opened in 1841, on the site of what was once the Blackfriars Monastery, with the construction of the chapel, coffins of the Blackfriars were found. The Blackfriars, also known as the Dominican or Preaching Friars, were in Lynn by 1271. Stepney Baptist Chapel is now Tawn & Landles.

There were also other friaries in Lynn, the Greyfrairs 1230, Augustin Friars in the reign of Edward I, White/Carmelites Friars 1260, Benedictine Priory was attached to St. Margarets. The Friars of the Sack, being few in number joined into other friaries. The Friaries were all dissolved in 1538 during the reign of Henry VIII, known as the reformation.

Another building that was constructed on the site of the Blackfriars was the Athenaeum in 1854, in 1883 it was taken over and used as the Post Office until it was demolished in the 1930's. The Post Office of today built in 1939 now stands on the site.

Stepney Baptist Chapel. Courtesy of J. Walker.

The Athenaeum after being taken over by the Post Office. Courtesy of the Fenprint Collection.

Post Office, present day. In the background is King's Lynn Museum opened in 1904 in a converted Baptist Chapel.

Blackfriars Street before demolition in the late 1960's. Courtesy of James Tuck

Blackfriars Street, present day.

The Majestic Cinema in Tower Street opened on the 23rd May 1928. Declared open by the Mayor, the choir of Lynn's All Saints Church sang hymns. The first film show was "Ben Hur" starring Ramon Navarro.

ST. JAMES CHAPEL
& ST. JAMES PARK

ST. JAMES CHAPEL was built by Bishop Eborard who succeeded Bishop De Losinga, St. James was built prior to St. Nicholas, both being chapels of ease to St. Margarets Church.

In 1361 in the reign of Edward III the priests of the chapel would collect their holy water from the Gay (Gaywood River) at the East Gate, making their way through Websters Row (now Broad St) and along the south side of Damgate, (now part of Norfolk St). The priests from St. Nicholas Chapel would also collect their holy water in the same way but by passing along the north side of Damgate.

St. James Chapel in Tudor times was allowed to fall into disrepair, in 1597 the plague was in the town and the sick were sent there. In the late 1600's it was converted into a workhouse.

When the old workhouse tower collapsed in 1854, some of the paupers still remained in the part of the building still standing, others were sent to Welwick House in Union St. Two year later in 1856 the new St. James workhouse was opened in Extons Road.

In 1856 the site of the old workhouse was sold to Frederick Savage & Co. Following further purchases other premises were erected on the land, the Primitive Methodist Chapel in 1858 and its School in 1874, the County Court in 1864 and St. James Hall and Assembly Rooms 1887.

The Assembly Rooms were partly destroyed by fire in 1904 and rebuilt as the St. James Cinema in 1906 which was destroyed by fire in 1937.

The Royal Standard public house, was also on the site built about 1871, was closed in 1970, since demolished. Still on the site today are the Methodist Chapel, Church Rooms, Tax Office & car Park, the old County Court building used some years ago as offices now no longer in use.

In 1803 the Chapel's burial ground needed to be extended as in the 1590's 200 plague victims had been buried there. A field adjacent was obtained by the corporation, in 1805 this became known as the new St. James burial ground. A small circular consecrated chapel stood in the middle. The burial ground was closed in 1854. In 1855 the Hardwick Road cemetery was opened.

In 1889 all the gravestones were removed from the St. James Burial ground although many of those buried there did not have a memorial stone, none of the bodies were removed, the gravestones (some now in a very dilapidated condition) were placed in County Court Road beside St. James House which is now the Doctors' Surgery. However some human remains were uncovered when the Nursery School was built.

In 1901 it was decided to make the burial ground into a park, in 1903 the park was opened, we know it today as St. James Park.

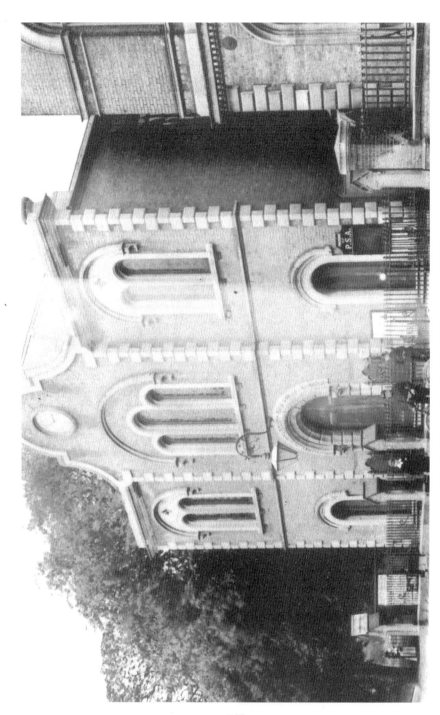

Methodist Chapel, London Road. Courtesy of J. Walker

Tombstones from the St. James Burial Ground.

The remains of the wall of the Workhouse. A plaque is on the wall beside the Medthodist Chapel.

St. James Theatre built in 1906 on the site of the Workhouse. Silent films were shown at St. James in 1914, known as the Picture Palace in 1921 and becoming Lynn's first cinema to show "talkies" in 1929.
Burnt down on 11th February 1937, now site of the Tax Office.

Early St. James Park. Courtesy of the Fenprint Collection.

Red Mount Chapel.

Red Mount Chapel, present day

View of Gaywood River, Red Mount in background.

Gaywood River flowing past the Bandstand.

Early Walks showing North Guanock Gate and Gaywood River. Courtesy of J. Walker.

North Guanock Gate.

Early Greyfriars Tower and St. James Street. Courtesy of the Fenprint Collection.

Greyfriars Tower, St. James Street.

Greyfriars Tower and War Memorial, Greyfriars Park. The small epitaph on the right is in tribute to the Burma Star Association.

The old cemetery cross from the Blackfriars Priory was rescued by E.M. Beloe and placed at first in Lynn Museum. It was then transferred to the Greenland Fishery and after being restored was placed in its present location beneath Greyfriars Tower in 1938. It is the only relic that remains of the Blackfriars.

Original Theatre built in 1815 in St. James Street. It was burnt down and replaced by the Theatre Royal and reopened in 1938. Courtesy of J. Walker.

163

Theatre Royal St. James Street now the Gala Club Bingo, present day.

GREENLAND FISHERY

The Greenland Fishery was originally the merchant house of John Atkin, Mayor of the Town in 1607.

Later part of the building became a public house, "The Watermans Arms" in 1736-38 and 1745. It became the Greenland Fishery in 1761.
Edward M. Beloe was instrumental in turning part of the building into a museum in 1912. The part of the building used as a public house was closed in 1921, it was also damaged by enemy bombing in 1941.

Greenland Fishery. Courtesy of J. Walker.

Greenland Fishery, present day.

View of St. Margarets Place, leading into Nelson Street. Valiant Sailor and Hampton Court in background.

Hampton Court.

Hanseatic Warehouse, St. Margarets Lane.

Hanseatic Warehouse.

St. Margarets Church. Courtesy of J. Walker.

St. Margarets Church.

Upper view of St. Margarets showing the clock and moonclock. Courtesy of Lynn News.

Moonclock, which shows the time of the tide.

Tombstones in St. Margarets Church at the back of Priory Cottages.

Early Town Hall.

Town Hall and Saturday Market Place.

Town Hall. Courtesy of Lynn News.

Clifton House, Queen Street. Courtesy of Lynn News.

Old Granary in Baker Lane. Now converted into flats.

Baker Lane flats, present day.

FLEETS & WATERWAYS

Many inlets or Fleets flowed throughout the Town, when looking at an old map one can see that the town was separated into tiny islands and totally surrounded by water, although many of the old fleets were piped and filled in 1865-66.

The Dowshill Fleet (or the old Fisher fleet) watercourse flowed across what we now know today as Austin Fields, it split into two tributaries, one flowed into the Gaywood river via a sluice at the old Kettle Mills. The other branch of the Dowshill Fleet passed under Hopmans Way to the Damgate fleet, flowing along Blackfriars road, it turned east where Eastgate school is and into the Gaywood river running under what is now Morrisons car park, into the river that runs behind the Red Mount. Dowshill fleet also flowed at the back of Gresemarket, Websters Row and Mercer Row, when the fleet was cleared of rubbish that had built up (this had to be done on a regular basis), it continued towards the Purfleet.

The Loke was a waterway that ran from the Fisher Fleet to the Kettle Mills. The Long Ponds either side of Loke Road were joined until the road was laid. The left hand pond has a sluice at the end which takes the water across Pecks Field to the Bawsey Drain, Clarkes Dyke as it is known is off Loke Road and part of the Bawsey Drain, but it also ran into the old Fisher Fleet via a sluice that can still be seen today. When the course of the river was altered in 1853, the Alexandra Dock was built on the reclaimed land and opened in 1869, with the building of the Bentinck Dock in 1883, the Loke was cut off causing it to become a stagnant pond. The Fisher Fleet that we know today is all that remains of the old Fisher Fleet.

The North Clow Fleet made its way from the Purfleet along the side of New Conduit Street , making its way under Baxters Bridge, beneath Clow Bridge and towards St Johns Walk, joining up with the river in the walks, another fleet from the Clow Bridge flowed westward towards Baxter Row St, and Fullers Row.

Whitefriars Fleet flowed down from Setch and Middleton on the south side of the town until it reached the river Great Ouse, Middleton Fleet went under the South Gates through Whitefriars and also flowed to the corn water mills, several of these water mills were in the town.

Another waterway was Colwaynes Fleet that once flowed into the town, (it was where Broad St. is now), it was piped in at a much earlier date.

The Millfleet flowed from Gaywood and Mintlyn via the Gaywood river to a sluice at the corner of Framlingham's almshouses on London Road, before mixing with the waters of the Great Ouse. The Millfleet was piped in from Ladybridge to London Road in 1898, it still continues to flow by the side of the Boal Quay.

The Purfleet waterway went under Wingate St., Briggate and Baxters Bridge, with this being the longest fleet it caused the most concern to the inhabitants of Lynn, it was an open drain like most of the others, where all manner of effluent was thrown into, with the insanitary and primitive conditions in which the people lived, this led to numerous outbreaks of cholera and typhoid, some of the dates are 1779-80, 1826, in 1831-32 King Cholera swept throughout the town, other dates are 1848 and 1854. Another epidemic that the residents of Lynn suffered from at various times was the Plague, some are in the years 1349, 1439, 1540, 1597 and the great plague in 1665, many lost their lives through this despicable disease, possibly carried by the crews of ships that came to the port.

The Fisher Fleet or Dowshill was another unsavoury waterway, where the inhabitants deposited almost everything into it, this led to a build up of waste along the muddy banks.

Lynn in those days must have been a very unhealthy place to live in, but somehow some of our ancestors survived. Not only were the inhabitants of the Town inflicted with diseases' they also endured storms and earthquakes, 1741 and 1779. Many years of flooding some being 1607, 1741, 1816, also in our modern time 1953 and 1978.

One date in particular was 1741, in that year the townspeople suffered catastrophic events. St. Nicholas Chapel and St. Margarets Spires were both blown down in the great storm. St. Margarets spire was never rebuilt, but St. Nicholas had a grand spire of lead replaced in 1871. The same spire that dominates the skyline of the town today.

WHARFS & LANDINGS 1577

Littleport Bridge in Damgate, one on East and West side of Dowshill bridge, St. Anns Yard, Page Stair Lane, Pudding Lane, Common Staithe Lane, Purfleet Wharf, King's Staithe, College Lane, Lath St., Whitefriars Bridge, Bevers Bridge, Baxters Bridge, Sedgeford Lane, Fincham St. and Little Checker.

CONDUITS

St. Margarets, New Conduit, Checker St., (King St.), Tuesday Market Conduit, St. Johns, and Littleport St.

NAMES OF OTHER FLEETS
Hewalde's Lane, Nickerefleet, Hewolne's Fleet, Ryflete and Surflete.

Purfleet before the North Sea Haven Millennium Project.

Purfleet before the North Sea Haven Project.

Mouth of the Purfleet before alteration.

Purfleet, present day after the North Sea Haven Millennium Project. Courtesy of Lynn News.

Purfleet Bridge and Custom House showing King Street.

Custom House and Purfleet. Built as a merchants house for Sir John Turner
in 1683, later the Custom House in 1718. Architect Henry Bell.

EXPLORERS OF KING'S LYNN

George Vancouver was born in the year 1757 in King's Lynn and he died in 1798. He was one of the famous men of Lynn, he was a navigator and explorer. He started his career in the Royal Navy serving with Captain Cook on two of his voyages. He was given command of H.M.S Discovery a fourteen gun sloop for an expedition to the Northwest coast of America. He discovered Vancouver Island which is named after him, there is a city in Canada which is also named after him.

He is honoured in King's Lynn by having Vancouver Avenue named after him. A statue of him has been erected on the Purfleet Quay.

A plaque is also on the Quay in honour of another famous man of Lynn, Friar Nicholas a Franciscan Greyfriar, a navigator, sailor, mathematician and astrologer who died in 1369. He made voyages to the America's long before Columbus, an expedition to Greenland in 1354 resulted in the Friars Map of Ancient America in 1360.

Purfleet showing statue of Captain George Vancouver, present day. Courtesy of Lynn News.

Vancouver's house before demolition.

Plaque on the Purfleet Quay of Friar Nicholas of Lynn.

The plaque reads:

FRIAR NICHOLAS OF LYNN
DIED 1369

VOYAGED TO ICELAND
REPUTED DISCOVERER OF THE AMERICAS

Other plaques on the Purfleet Quay of famous mariners.

Purfleet Street, present day.

Highbridge House, Purfleet Street.
Once occupied by the Lynn News offices.

197

BANK HOUSE
HOME OF ANOTHER SAILOR OF KING'S LYNN

Lieutenant Samuel Cresswell was a grandson of Elizabeth Fry the prison reformer, who was the daughter of John Gurney. Elizabeth married Joseph Fry, their daughter Rachel married Captain Francis Cresswell who's son Samuel was born in 1827.

He joined the Royal Navy, and when under the command of Captain Robert McClure they voyaged to the coast of Alaska via the Bering Strait in search of Sir John Franklin, who had undertaken an expedition to discover the Northwest Passage. After being unable to find any trace of Franklin they had to abandon their ship when it became trapped in the ice. (Franklin was never found alive). Lt. Cresswell with some other men undertook the journey across the frozen waste, luckily they were found and returned to Great Britain.

On his return to King's Lynn a banquet was given in his honour, he was also bestowed with the freedom of the borough. The years he had spent in the arctic conditions had taken a toll on his health and he died at the Bank House in 1867 aged 39.

Rachel Cresswell later lived in the new bank's premises on the Tuesday Market Place, the bank we know today as Barclays Bank. She died in 1888.

Bankhouse, King Staithe Square.

Early South Quay. Courtesy of the Fenprint Collection.

Ship leaving South Quay.

South Quay with views of river and silos which no longer exist.

South Quay, present day.

Early Boal Quay showing Pauls Mill. Courtesy of the Fenprint Collection.

Pauls Mill chimney on Boal Quay was demolished, site is now a car park.

St. Georges Guildhall, King Street, when used by G.M. Bridges scenic artists in 1920. Now the King's Lynn Arts Centre.

St. Georges Guildhall, now the Arts Centre, present day.

BIBLIOGRAPHY

Hillen : History of Lynn 1909

W. Taylor. : Guide to King's Lynn 1848.

Holcombe Ingleby. : The Treasures Of Lynn 1924.